THE PROTECTION OF
RELIGIOUS MINORITIES
WORLDWIDE

*A Symposium Organized by
Pax Romana at the United Nations and
the United Nations Alliance of Civilizations*

DEAN ELIZABETH F. DEFEIS

&

PETER F. O'CONNOR

Editors

PACEM IN TERRIS PRESS

www.paceminterrispress.net

ISBN-13: 978-1518732065
ISBN-10: 1518732062

*Opinions or claims expressed in publications
from Pacem in Terris Press represent the opinions and claims of the books' authors and
do not necessarily represent the official position of Pacem in Terris Press
or its sponsor or of any officials of the Press or its sponsor.*

PACEM IN TERRIS PRESS
is the publishing arm of the
PACEM IN TERRIS GLOBAL LEADERSHIP INITIATIVE.
The Initiative is sponsored by

PAX ROMANA
Catholic Movement for Intellectual & Cultural Affairs
USA
1025 Connecticut Avenue NW, Suite 1000, Washington DC 20036
www.pax-romana-cmica-usa.org

PAX ROMANA AT THE UNITED NATIONS
*is a project of the New York City Chapter of Pax Romana / Catholic
Movement for Intellectual & Cultural Affairs USA*

WITH GRATITUDE TO THE GENEROUS DONORS

WHO MADE THIS SYMPOSIUM POSSIBLE

SOVEREIGN MILITARY ORDER OF MALTA

BARONESSA FLAVIA FRATI-SPAGNOLA

MS. LAURA HAGAN

MS. ASTRID HORAN

MS. PRUE KENNY

MS. UDA KLEE

MS. VICTORIA NEWHOUSE

DEDICATION

*Pax Romana at the United Nations dedicates this publication
to the countless persons, belonging to religious minorities,
who have been killed, injured, or marginalized
as a result of religious intolerance.*

MAKE ME AN INSTRUMENT OF PEACE;

WHERE THERE IS HATRED, LET ME SOW LOVE;

WHERE THERE IS INJURY, PARDON;

WHERE THERE IS ERROR, TRUTH;

WHERE THERE IS DOUBT, FAITH;

WHERE THERE IS DESPAIR, HOPE;

WHERE THERE IS DARKNESS, LIGHT;

AND WHERE THERE IS SADNESS, JOY.

Attributed to
SAINT FRANCIS OF ASSISI

PAX ROMANA AT THE UNITED NATIONS
*is a project of the New York City Chapter of Pax Romana / Catholic
Movement for Intellectual & Cultural Affairs USA*

SYMPOSIUM ON THE PROTECTION

OF RELIGIOUS MINORITIES WORLDWIDE

Held on
13 November 2014 in the
United Nations Economic and Social Council Chamber

Organized by
Pax Romana at the United Nations[1]
and the United Nations Alliance of Civilizations

Sponsored by
The Permanent Mission of Italy
The Permanent Observer Mission of the Holy See
The Permanent Mission of the Hashemite Kingdom of Jordan
The Permanent Mission of the Philippines
The Sovereign Military Order of Malta

Focused on
Discussion of means of protecting religious minorities
and the role of the international community, national governments,
and faith-based organizations, as well as religious and political leaders in promoting religious pluralism and religious freedom
as an inherent human right

A video of the Symposium is available at
http://webtv.un.org/watch/symposium-on-the-protection-of-religious-minori-
ties-worldwide-unaoc-pax-romana/3890706621001

---

[1] "Pax Romana at the United Nations" is a project of the New York City Chapter of Pax
Romana / Catholic Movement for Intellectual & Cultural Affairs - USA

TABLE OF CONTENTS

INTRODUCTION

MR. FRANCIS DUBOIS

*Former United Nations Deputy Coordinator to the Palestinian
Territories and Head of the United Nations Offices in
Algeria, Iraq, and Tunisia*

and

DR. JOSEF KLEE

*Former United Nations Official
Director, Pax Romana at the United Nations*

T hroughout history, religious minorities have experienced discrimination, persecution, expulsion, and genocide. After the Second World War with the creation of the United Nations, there were great hopes that all peoples could live in peace with one another as good neighbors, based on the fundamental human rights and the practice of tolerance as stated in the Preamble of the UNITED NATIONS CHARTER.

Need for Effective UN Strategies

However, the United Nations never developed specific and effective strategies to protect the human rights of religious minorities and to stop their persecution, expulsion and genocide.

The United Nations adopted several rather weak legal mechanisms to address religious discrimination, namely international instruments with little or no enforcement mechanism such as Article 18 of the UNIVERSAL DECLARATION OF HUMAN RIGHTS and the creation of the Special Rapporteur on Freedom of Religion and Belief.

Article 18 stipulates that:

> *"Everyone shall have the right to freedom of thought, conscience and religion; this right includes freedom to change his religion or belief, and freedom, either alone or in community with others and in public or private, to manifest his religion or belief in teaching, practice, worship and observance."*

The United Nations – for obvious political reasons – has never been able to adopt and implement measures to monitor or enforce the adherence by Member States of the provisions of Article 18.

The United Nations Commission on Human Rights – based on Article 18 – has established the position of the Special Rapporteur on Freedom of Religion or Belief. The position is occupied by an independent expert who serves part-time and does not have any support staff. The mandate of the Rapporteur is limited to the identification of obstacles to the free exercise of belief and to making recommendations for overcoming those obstacles.

So far, the work of the Special Rapporteur has not proven to be effective, since the Rapporteur's investigation methods are limited to country visits and to preparing reports on findings. In the Rapporteur's his last press conference on 24 October 2014, the Rapporteur expressed his frustrations with the limitations of the work.

In the last decade, the world has witnessed an unprecedented increase in violent persecution of religious minorities, particularly in the Middle East, in Asia and in Africa. The international community has been a bystander and has not been able or willing to develop a strategy to protect persecuted minorities and to stop their expulsion and genocide. However, one must recognize that the United Nations has been providing humanitarian assistance to refugees who fled for religious reasons.

"Pax Romana at the United Nations"

For several years, our *"Pax Romana at the United Nations"* group has observed with great concern the desperate plight religious minorities. Several of our members worked as United Nations officials in regions with religious minorities, and thus have first-hand knowledge of their tragic situation.

Our group is trying to raise awareness of the plight of persecuted people, to advocate for international measures to protect religious minorities and to provide assistance to religious refugees. We do this by publishing articles, giving speeches, issuing press releases, etc. The United Nations Symposium the Protection of Religious Minorities Worldwide, organized on 14 November 2014 at the United Nations Headquarters is one example of our efforts.

"Pax Romana at the United Nations" is part of the worldwide Pax Romana movement, which is one of the oldest international lay Catholic movements. It was created in two stages with two branches: first, in 1921, as a lay movement of Catholic University students; and second, in 1947, as a lay movement of Catholic intellectuals and professionals.

The first branch is called in English the "International Movement of Catholic Students" (IMCS), and the second branch is called in English the "International Catholic Movement for Intellectual and Cultural Affairs" (ICMICA). Both branches work together to serve the need to build a peaceful and just world.

Pax Romana, the name that both branches share in common, referred originally to the peace for which its leaders worked in cooperation with the papacy after World War I. The name was given to the movement in 1921 by Pope Benedict XV, when he reportedly said to its leaders "you are my *Pax Romana*."

Pax Romana, as both movements working in partnership, has the highest level of consultative status with the Economic and Social Council of the United Nations. It maintains NGO (nongovernmental organizational) representatives at U.N. offices in New York, Paris, Geneva, Vienna and Nairobi. It is also a member of CONGO (Committee of NGOs having official relationship with United Nations). In addition, for the Canon Law of the

4

Catholic Church, Pax Romana is recognized as a private organization and it is accredited to the Pontifical Council for the Laity of the Holy See ("Vatican").

To assist the work of the global Pax Romana movement at the United Nations in New York, Pax Romana / Catholic Movement for Intellectual and Cultural Affairs – USA (CMICA), a U.S. federation of ICMICA, sponsors its New York Office for the United Nations. *"Pax Romana at the United Nations"* is the core project of this New York Office. The project offers its services to assist the work of IMCS and ICMICA representatives on the Pax Romana NGO team at the United Nations in New York.

Pax Romana / CMICA–USA also sponsors a U.N.-oriented and semester-long internship for law students from St. Thomas University School of Law in Miami Gardens, Florida. This program is directed by Dr. Mark Wolf, Professor of Law at St. Thomas University School of Law. Additionally, Dr. Wolf is currently an NGO representative of Pax Romana at the United Nations in New York. Students in the law-internship program are assigned legal work in United Nations offices, in offices of member-state missions at the United Nations, and in offices of intergovernmental and non-governmental organizations accredited to the U.N.

Further, our *"Pax Romana at the United Nations"* project sponsors in New York City an ongoing seminar for UN-related individuals interested in Catholic Social Teaching. This seminar meets one evening per month for prayer, study, and dialogue.

Conclusion

In conclusion, we are pleased that the 2014 Symposium at the United Nations in New York on the "Protection of Religious Minorities Worldwide," was successful. We are equally proud that this collection of papers from the Symposium is being published. And we thank the many people who made both this Symposium and the book possible.

Further, we are extremely grateful to the United Nations High Representative for the Alliance of Civilizations, Ambassador Al Nasser, for having sponsored this event.

Lastly, we hope that the international community will acknowledge the dire situation of so many religious minorities and will adopt practical strategies and measures for protection and strong humanitarian assistance of the expelled religious refugees.

2

OPENING REMARKS

HIS EXCELLENCY, NASSIR ABDULAZIZ AL-NASSER

High Representative
United Nations Alliance of Civilizations

E xcellencies, Ladies and Gentlemen, Distinguished Guests. Let me start by saying that I am very pleased to convene this symposium co-organized with Pax Romana on a timely subject that addresses key issues that challenge minority communities, in particular religious minorities and States in all regions.

Important UN Documents

The rights of minorities and the principles of non-discrimination are inherent in the UN CHARTER and various international treaties and declarations. Foremost among these is the UNITED NATIONS DECLARATION ON THE RIGHTS OF PERSONS BELONGING TO NATIONAL, ETHNIC, RELIGIOUS AND LINGUISTIC MINORITIES. In 2012 we celebrated the 20th Anniversary of the adoption by all

Member States at the General Assembly in 1992 of this essential declaration, which marked a global recognition that the rights of minorities everywhere must be respected, protected and promoted in the face of continuing violations of the rights of those belonging to certain communities.

As a major United Nations instrument that specifically addressed the special rights of minorities, the DECLARATION can be viewed as a point of reference for the international community. Yet, much remains to be done to make the rights stipulated in this DECLARATION A reality. Today, many ethnic and religious minorities continue to face discrimination, marginalization and exclusion, let alone systematic persecution in some countries that amount to crimes against humanity.

In that respect, the United Nations is all too aware of the dangers of intolerance when it comes to minority populations. The United Nations Secretary General has taken up this cause saying:

> *The United Nations' work to promote tolerance is fundamental to both conflict prevention and peace-building. Without tolerance, our work on development and good governance would achieve little.*

Allow me to remind you of the 2005 WORLD SUMMIT OUTCOME DOCUMENT, issued by the same world gathering that re-affirmed the role of United Nations Alliance of Civilizations ("UNAOC") as a platform for dialogue. In that document, all Heads of State and Government committed to protect their populations from genocide, war crimes, ethnic cleansing and crimes against humanity – including their incitement, and to provide assistance to states under stress to fulfill their responsibilities towards their populations.

In that sense, the United Nations Alliance of Civilizations (UNAOC) takes these facts seriously when conducting its mission, since minorities are the vulnerable parties who become the subject of discrimination and xenophobia. This is where the four pillars of the UNAOC come into play, namely: Youth, Education, Media and Migration.

Threats to Religious Minorities

In today's globalized world, multi-ethnic communities and religious pluralism weave the fabric of our diverse societies. Sadly, some myths resist reality and a majority group or a dominant religion or culture in countries around the world seek to impose their beliefs or identity on other groups who are a minority. I see a world today grappling with a rising wave of hostility and extremism, and this poses serious threats to the establishment, promotion and advancement of the post-2015 Development Agenda; especially to the eleventh and sixteenth goals of the Sustainable Development Goals ("SDG"). I cannot stress enough the fact that peace-and-security and sustainable development are a two-way relationship.

Hostility towards the other is manifested in demonstrating intolerance and extremism that escalates to violence, and too often, to systematic persecution. The innocent victims of such criminal acts are usually the vulnerable populations, including religious minorities. Sectarian violence is dividing societies, fueling violent conflicts and feeding the furnace of intolerance.

Extremists and radical ideologues misuse religion and incite hatred to foster hostility towards other minorities who embrace different beliefs or faiths. By doing so, those fundamentalists contradict the most sacred tenets of sacred faiths. None of the existing faiths advocate for violence or intolerance.

On the other hand, at the State level, a growing number of governments are imposing restrictions on religious beliefs and practices by minority religious groups, hence nurturing a conflict-ridden environment and enflaming sectarianism.

Wherever communities believe they face persistent discrimination, humiliation, or marginalization based on ethnic, religious or other identity markers, they are likely to assert their identity more aggressively. This is where we see those who try to enflame the feelings of resentment and collective anger.

I ask the question: What can be done? There is a lot of work ahead of us. But let us first agree to the notion that intolerance and violence are obstacles to peace and security in any given society and in the world where we all live. Governments, the international community, religious and political leaders have a shared responsibility to confront and curb hostility towards minorities.

Good governance plays a vital role in including minorities in societies and protecting their rights and interests. States should contribute to the elimination of negative stereotypes against individuals on the basis of their religion or belief, in particular members of religious minorities.

Education programmes, awareness-raising campaigns, monitoring and preventing hate speech, inter-religious and inter-cultural dialogue initiatives can help broaden horizons towards an appreciation of the real diversity and creativity of human beings in this universe.

Role of Alliance of Civilizations

I would like to take a moment to explain how this relates to the work and the mission of the United Nations Alliance of Civilizations. The Alliance is one entity in the United Nations that is particularly devoted to fostering inter-cultural and inter-religious dialogue and promoting tolerance. We strive to achieve this goal through wide-ranging approaches to our four pillars which, as I mentioned earlier, with the added priorities of sport, music and the arts.

Recognizing the vital role of religious leaders and faith-based organizations in promoting tolerance and curbing incitement, we at the UNAOC are now working more closely with relevant UN departments and agencies to ensure that the voices of faith-based communities are heard when we discuss these controversial topics. We continue to work to bring more religious leaders into the mainstream of the United Nations' activities around conflict resolution and mediation.

When it comes to media, the modern media is a source of information for many people. This industry can, therefore, greatly influence public opinion and shape perceptions. Media can be used as a propaganda machine presenting a distorted view of particular issues, thus fueling hatred and violence. It can also play a constructive role. For that reason, we have been particularly active in skill-building with training for media professionals. We had recently launched a media-friendly glossary on the coverage of migration, thus providing journalists covering migration and migrant-related culturally sensitive issues with a viable tool. By doing so, the UNAOC is contributing to strengthening discussions among media professionals on ways of improving standards of reporting to avoid intolerance and hate speech towards minorities. We are now in the early stages of developing a project on monitoring hate speech and incitement.

The UNAOC has developed programs that ensure a diversity of voices and free quality content. We continue to create opportunities for young men and women to launch for-profit social enterprises, and empower youth by educating them on the values of tolerance, diversity and respect of the other, therefore, providing them with opportunities to be leaders of social change within their own communities. Our initiatives are based on the conviction that youth are the driving force for change, and education, formal and non-formal is the ultimate short, medium and long-term solution to secure lasting change in the future.

Let me conclude by re-affirming that the protection of religious minorities worldwide is an integral part of the protection of human rights. It is our collective responsibility, as international community, governments, Non-Government Organizations, religious and political leaders and educational institutions to collaborate together to achieve this goal.

3

REFLECTIONS BY THE APOSTOLIC NUNCIO

TO THE UNITED NATIONS

HIS EXCELLENCY, ARCHBISHOP BERNARDITO AUZA

Apostolic Nuncio, Permanent Observer Mission
of the Holy See to the United Nations

Y our Excellency Nassir Abdulaziz Al-Nasser, the United
Nations' High Representative for the Alliance of Civilizations, Dr. Josef Klee, representing Pax Romana, Distinguished
Panelists, Mr. Moderator, Francis Dubois, Your Excellencies, Ladies and Gentlemen:

At the very outset, I wish to thank the United Nations Alliance
of Civilizations and Pax Romana for organizing this symposium
on the protection of religious minorities worldwide.

This is a burning issue, and thus highly relevant. In many parts of the world, religious minorities are continuously subjected to violations of their fundamental human rights, simply because of their religion and religious belief.

It is for this reason that Pope Francis reiterated his appeal to those who have political responsibility both on a local and on an international level, as well as to all persons of goodwill, to engage in a vast mobilization of consciences on the plight of persecuted Christians and of all minorities who are denied their fundamental human rights for religious reasons.

This symposium responds to this appeal, as it intends to sensitize us to the extremely difficult situations that religious minorities are facing in many parts of the world, in spite of the laudable effort of institutions and individuals.

Looming large in our preoccupations is the outright persecution of the ethnic and religious minorities, including the Christian communities, in northern Iraq by the so-called Islamic State of Iraq and the Levant ("ISIL"). Their treatment of the minorities, as well as so many of those in the majority religion who do not agree with their own interpretation of the religious texts, violate the most fundamental human rights. Their intolerance and brutal deeds in the name of religion speak eloquently of the tremendous harm that distortion of religion can do to people and to religion itself.

The Holy See insists that these ruthless violations must not only be seen as violence against ethnic and religious minorities, but first and foremost must be condemned as blatant violations of fundamental human rights, and must be dealt with accordingly.

The Holy See calls on the competent organs of the United Nations to act to prevent possible new massacres of defenseless religious and ethnic minorities. Along this line, the United Nations should re-enforce the international juridical framework of a multilateral application of the responsibility to protect people from genocide, war crimes, ethnic cleansing, crimes against humanity and all forms of unjust aggression.

With lessons learned from a failure to stop recent horrors of genocide due to ethnic and religious intolerance, and presently confronted with clear, massive violations of fundamental human rights and of international humanitarian law, the time is for courageous decisions.

Finally, this symposium should serve to remind religious and civic leaders of their grave responsibility to foster respect for religious minorities and avoid fomenting discrimination and violence against them. As a cleric myself, I wish to reiterate the call of the Pope to all the religious leaders everywhere in the world to play a leading role in promoting interreligious and intercultural dialogue, in promptly denouncing every misuse of religion to justify violent extremism, and in educating all to reciprocal understanding and mutual respect.

Moreover, all of us must assume this responsibility to practice openness, dialogue and sincere acceptance of the ethnic or religious minorities in our midst. This is especially true and urgently needed in those countries and regions where religious minorities, even at this very moment, are discriminated against and persecuted.

A world that truly respects religious freedom must move beyond mere toleration to a lived conviction that, as the Universal Declaration of Human Rights and international human rights instruments explicitly affirm.

> *Everyone has the right to freedom of thought, conscience and religion ... [and' this right includes freedom to change his or her religion or belief, and freedom, either alone or in community with others and in public or private, to manifest his or her religion or belief in teaching, practice, worship and observance.*

It includes as well the freedom not to believe.

I am sure that our panelists will provide us ample information and reflection on this problem that plagues the human family today.

4

PAX ROMANA

INTRODUCTORY STATEMENT

DR. MARK J. WOLFF

Pax Romana Representative to the United Nations

and

DR. EDWARD "JOE" HOLLAND, III

President of Pax Romana / Cmica-usa

P ax Romana / Catholic Movement for Intellectual & Cultural Affairs - USA is a strong advocate for human rights especially when it comes to the right to practice freedom of religion.

We express our profound appreciation and gratitude to Ambassador Al-Naseer the High Representative for U.N. Alliance of Civilization, and also to the organizers of this important initiative, as well as to the sponsors of the event, namely, the Permanent Mission of Italy, the Permanent Observer Mission of the Holy See, the Permanent Mission of the Hashemite Kingdom of Jordan, the Permanent Mission of the Philippines, and the Knights of Malta.

The worldwide movement of Pax Romana has long been devoted to freedom of religion across the globe. For example, Pax Romana / Cmica-usa national chaplain at the time, Rev. John Courtney Murray SJ, played an important role in the drafting of the DECLARATION ON RELIGIOUS FREEDOM, DIGNITATIS HUMANAE, produced by the Second Ecumenical Council of the Vatican and promulgated by his Holiness Pope Paul VI on 7 December 1965.

In addition on 30 March 2011 and in partnership with St. Thomas University School of Law in Miami Gardens, Florida, the Main Representative of Pax Romana to the United Nations, Professor Mark J. Wolff, organized a symposium on persecution of Christians in the Middle East.

More recently on 9 September 2013, the Pax Romana / Cmica-usa New York Office for the United Nations, directed by Dr. Josef Klee and Francis Dubois, issued a statement of concern about the growing persecution of Christians and other religious minorities across the world.

We sincerely hope that this important symposium being held today will become a fertile seed for expanding the concern of the United Nations, of governments across the world, and of leaders of every major world religion, for the protection and defense of all religious minorities wherever they may be found.

5

CONCEPT PAPER AND

OUTLINE OF THE SYMPOSIUM

Ms. Nihal Saad

Office of the High Representative
United Nations Alliance of Civilizations

T he concept of non-discrimination lies at the heart of human rights. There exists a whole range of rights-based international treaties adopted under the auspices of the United Nations that affirm the right to equality and non-discrimination.

The international community now recognizes that it is not sufficient merely to ensure that there is no discrimination against minorities. Special measures are essential to protect and promote the rights of minorities, particularly those pertinent to preserving minorities' identity and culture.

As such, the international community adopted the UNITED NATIONS DECLARATION ON THE RIGHTS OF PERSONS BELONGING TO NATIONAL, ETHNIC, RELIGIOUS AND LINGUISTIC MINORITIES (Minorities Declaration) in 1992 and subsequently created the U.N. Sub-Commission Working Group on Minorities. Yet, despite these efforts, discrimination is still rampant. Violence perpetrated against religious minorities is escalating in many parts of the world.

Minorities in many regions of the world continue to face serious threats, discrimination and racism and are frequently excluded from taking part fully in the economic, social, political and cultural life in the countries where they live. Achieving effective participation of minorities and ending their exclusion requires that we embrace diversity through promotion and implementation of international human rights and standards.

Moreover, recent dramatic events involving atrocities committed against religious minorities from Iraq and Nigeria to Pakistan, Sri Lanka and Myanmar have further aggravated the situation. In many places, religious minorities have been forced to flee from their homes and witness the destruction of their places of worship and religious patrimony.

The significant escalation in tensions between groups of different beliefs or religions, often resulting in violence, are conducive to a possible risk of genocide or crimes against humanity. In many cases, hate speech and incitement to hatred have contributed to intolerance and violence against minorities.

States have the primary responsibility to protect their populations by preventing atrocities committed against minorities, including their incitement. Likewise, the International Community has a responsibility to assist States in meeting these responsibilities towards their populations. In that context, religious leaders have an essential role to play in promoting tolerance and preventing incitement and hate speech.

As such, interfaith dialogue initiatives launched in recent years are contributing to mutual knowledge, understanding and respect among communities finding ways to build common ground for more harmonious relations between individuals and communities.

This Symposium, organized by the United Nations Alliance of Civilization and Pax Romana, while affirming religious pluralism and religious freedom as an inherent human right issue, will focus on discussing means of protecting religious minorities and the role of the international community, national governments, and faith-based organizations as well as religious and political leaders towards that end.

6

A RELIGIOUS PERSPECTIVE ON

PERSECUTION OF RELIGIOUS MINORITIES

RABBI ROGER ROSS

Chairman of the Board & Chief Financial Officer
New Vision Interspiritual Seminary

Y our Excellencies, distinguished panel and guests, my dear brothers and sisters. It is truly an honor to be joining you here today to speak to the protection of religious minorities worldwide.

I do not believe that anyone here does not believe that religious minorities need our protection when and where their very existence is threatened. It is not as if each of our faiths was never in the minority nor felt the injustice of that. Throughout history, all religions have, at one time or another, been in the minority.

As we choose to enter this arena, we have to check our personal prejudices at the door. All faiths deserve our support, and all faiths must be accorded the same level of protection. All of us, whether we be Jews, Christians, Muslims, Hindus or any other of the myriad religions practiced today, are commanded by individual conscience, as well as by the laws of governments and our respective faiths, to respect and protect the rights of all of our fellow human beings.

As a spiritual human being, I believe that there is good and evil, and in the battle for the souls of all humans, evil will use false accusations against the weakest minority to remove one obstacle after another in its rise to power. It is only when we, who are spiritually aligned with the light of good, and open the eyes of the world to the horror of these actions can we bring more light into the world, and save more lives from the onslaught of evil.

Regardless of the differences of color, ethnicity or creed, it will be the spiritual dimension of humans that may, at last, put an end to any of these oppressions. There should be no question that religious leaders must lead – lead the effort to stand against the destruction of minorities and all the horror that brings.

His Holiness, the Dalai Lama said, "I appreciate any organization or individual people who sincerely make an effort to promote harmony among humanity, and particularly harmony among the various religions. I consider it very sacred work and very important work."

So we, rabbis, imams, priests, ministers and guides of all other faiths, may not see ourselves as religious leaders because we assume that only those with a world stage presence can identify themselves as such. But we are leaders to 10 or 100 or 1,000 people within our own communities and so we can use our small world stage to bring this message to huge numbers of people.

One of the most important duties for all clergy is to be firmly and publicly against the persecution of those of a minority faith. To speak up no matter where or when or what danger we may face from those committing atrocities against religious minorities.

Each of us was created with the same gifts, the gifts of life and the gift of love, and each of us was instructed to love and support our fellow human beings. We who profess to be leaders in our faiths, in our communities, and in our ability to influence for the good, must seek justice for all those who are experiencing or who have experienced attacks on their religion.

Dr. Gregory H. Stanton, the president of Genocide Watch wrote that there are several stages that contribute to the destructive impulse of vilifying minorities, and I would like to use some of what he wrote:

> All cultures have categories to distinguish people into 'us and them' by their religion. The main preventive measure is to develop universalistic institutions that transcend religious divisions and that actively promote acceptance and understanding. We give names or other symbols to the classifications of others, and distinguish them in a derogatory way by colors or dress; and apply those symbols to members of groups. At this very first step is the moment when we religious, political and

educational leaders must integrate interfaith and inter-spir-
itual education, before the inexorable onset of the very concept
that destroying another's religion is permissible.

Because we as leaders speak to so many people in our congregations and in our communities, we have the opportunity and responsibility to make using symbolization simply another way of seeing differences in a loving and accepting way. When we don't step up and offer an alternative view, one group will deny the humanity of another group, and use that as a reason to destroy those labeled as "other."

Here we must take the stand that every group of human beings, and every choice of religion is equal to any other, and we must teach that love and acceptance will erase even the thoughts of vilification, or suffer the same fate as Pastor Martin Niemoller of Berlin, who wrote:

First they came for the Socialists, and I did not speak out
— Because I was not a Socialist.

Then they came for the Trade Unionists, and I did not speak out
— Because I was not a Trade Unionist.

Then they came for the Jews, and I did not speak out
— Because I was not a Jew.

Then they came for me
— and there was no one left to speak for me.

And so, we have a responsibility to emphasize the fact that we are not intrinsically different — that we were all created equally by the Divine of our understanding. The lesson must be that we are all children of the One Divine, and not one of us is different from the other. Our clothing or color or ethnicity may be different from some of our brothers and sisters, but that is only the wrapping and is not the true essence of each, which is, we find as we study, exactly the same as our own.

If we learn, through inter-faith and inter-spiritual education, to look and really see – we too will realize that each faith, and each human being that professes that faith, is a unique and sacred part of the whole scheme of existence. We will begin to remember that, beneath the words we have heard before from those who hate, the truth is there for us to see and learn. It is important to repeat and remember that each of us was created with the same gifts – the gifts of life and love – and each of us was instructed to love and support our fellow human beings.

In the Torah of Judaism it is written that, if a man from another country is living in your land with you, do not make life hard for him; let him be to you as one of your countrymen, and have love for him as for yourself; for once you were living in a strange land, in the land of Egypt.

In my faith, we learn that Judaism teaches involvement and concern with the plight of fellow human beings. Every life is sacred, and we are obligated to do what we can to help others. The Torah states: "You shall not stand idly by the blood of your brother" (Lev. 19:16). What better message – what better instruction – then to take a stand for total loving allowance and personal responsibility to end the pattern of divisiveness and hate?

The Palestine Mandate of 1922 contained a number of provisions ensuring freedom of religion and conscience and protection of holy places, as well as prohibiting discrimination on religious grounds. Further, the Palestine Order in Council of that same year provided that "all persons ... shall enjoy full liberty of conscience and the free exercise of their forms of worship, subject only to the maintenance of public order and morals." It also lays down that "no ordinance shall be promulgated which shall restrict complete freedom of conscience and the free exercise of all forms of worship."

A. Powell Davies, an American minister, wrote: "True religion, like our founding principles, requires that the rights of the disbeliever be equally acknowledged with those of the believer."

In his work MUSLIMS AND NON-MUSLIMS, FACE-TO-FACE, Ahmad Sakr has written:

> This is a message from Muhammad ibn Abdullah, as a covenant to those who adopt Christianity, near and far, we are with them. Verily I, the servants, the helpers, and my followers defend them, because Christians are my citizens. No compulsion is to be on them.

The individual believer has often been the target of oppression for thinking or speaking anything that is perceived as other than orthodox thoughts, for assembling with those of other faiths, or for changing their religious affiliation. Typically, the aggressors have been large religious groups. Freedom from such oppression is religious freedom, religious liberty, freedom of worship and freedom to worship.

Throughout the ages, it has been said that many of the most horrific wars have been fought in the name of God. Those who lead their countries to war do it for power, possessions, and wealth, but the "common" people of these countries are convinced that it is a war of one faith against another. If only there was a way to teach the people the truth. The truth is that there is only One Divine Being and that we are all children of that Divinity.

The call to war has usually included the words, "God is on our side," and that statement has been used to justify the killing or enslaving anyone who prays differently or follows any path that appears to be different. The wars in Africa, the World Trade Center attack, the conflict between Israelis and Palestinians, the conflicts in Northern Ireland, the Balkans, Chechnya and everywhere else in the world have usually been labeled a "Holy War" and included some form of ethnic cleansing that followed religious lines.

The simple truth is that when there is the destruction of a minority, in the end, there are no winners, only losers who suffer the loss of their humanity – the loss of their souls. Destroying a minority religion devours everything – those who call themselves winners are merely the next to be devoured.

Kindness and compassion appear to be in short supply these days in spite of the fact that all of the world's faith traditions call upon their followers to choose that path. And, it is because of this lack that some people are moved to violence and to taking the life of another.

As Eleanor Roosevelt so wisely said: "We have to face the fact that either all of us are going to die together, or we are going to learn to live together; and if we are to live together, we have to talk."

Perhaps, in the spirit of respect, understanding, compassion and kindness, kindled by the effort to talk to each other and to understand and respect each other, there will no longer be any taking of life, and we will fulfill the plan that the God of our understanding (or the good of our understanding) put into motion at the beginning of creation. Perhaps, as partners with the Divine of our understanding, we religious leaders will speak out and remind every person that each of our faiths demands love and not hatred.

Then we would see faith in action, faith that is unrestricted, faith that is inclusive. Faith that recognizes our oneness in this world and the greatness of our Creator, however we choose to understand that Creator.

Closed-minded religions and religious communities create separation, and we must support the rights of those labeled nonbelievers who are in a minority and who are identified by their religions as "other" and are being oppressed. By doing so, we remove the power of the need to identify one's self at the expense of the "other" and to end the focus on the conflicting rights of majorities and minorities.

We can stop identifying all religions as different groups who cannot or will not share the same space and share in the power of self-determination. If all would remember, "there but for the grace of the Divine of my understanding go I," in my humble opinion, it's a good possibility that sectarian violence against minority faith groups would finally be a thing of the past.

Rabbi Harold Kushner prayed the following:

Let the rain come and wash away the ancient grudges and bitter hatreds held and nurtured over generations. Let the rain wash away the memory of the hurt, the neglect. Then let the sun come out and fill the sky with rainbows. Let the warmth of the sun heal us wherever we are broken. Let it burn away the fog so that we can see each other clearly, so that we can see beyond labels, beyond accents, gender or skin color. Let the warmth and brightness of the sun melt our selfishness, so that we can share the joys and feel the sorrows of our neighbors. And let the sun be so strong that we will see all people as our neighbors. Let the earth, nourished by rain, bring forth flowers to surround us with beauty. And let the mountains teach our hearts to reach upward to heaven.

I believe that to be one, to be united, is a great thing, but to respect the right of everyone else to be different is even greater.

7

THE HUMANITARIAN CRISIS
OF EXPELLED RELIGIOUS MINORITIES

DR. JEMILAH MAHMOOD

Director, World Humanitarian Summit,
United Nations Office for Coordination of Humanitarian Affairs

W e live in a world where crisis, disaster and vulnerability are becoming the norm. At this moment, the United Nations estimates that 6.5 million Syrians are internally displaced and a total of 9.3 million people are in need of humanitarian assistance – 46 percent of whom are children. In the Central African Republic, nearly 10 percent of the total population are internally displaced, and an estimated 2.5 million people need humanitarian assistance – nearly half the population of the Central African Republic. Around the world, over 100 million people are in need of urgent, life-saving humanitarian intervention; that is the equivalent of one out of every three people in the United States, or the entire population of the Philippines.

Today's crises challenge old assumptions about conflict, risk and vulnerability. This is one of the reasons why the United Nations Secretary-General has called for the first ever World Humanitarian Summit in 2016, hosted by Turkey. It is to challenge our assumptions and propose big changes that are needed to help the most vulnerable people better cope with the impact of crises.

Challenging Trends

In the lead-up to the World Humanitarian Summit 2016, it is important for us to not only understand where we have come from, but to look to the future and understand where we are going.

What are the trends that will dominate the humanitarian sphere in 10, 20, or 30 years' time? How can we act today in order to save lives and protect people tomorrow?

Conflicts presently account for around 85 percent of humanitarian needs. The number and intensity of armed conflicts are not likely to diminish in the next 15 years, and resource scarcity may even cause conflicts to increase, meaning that conflicts are likely to continue to create immense humanitarian needs.

While development has a clear impact on mitigating the consequences of natural disasters, development gains do not translate to conflict prevention. As we have witnessed with the Syria crisis, conflicts do not only take place in the world's poorest countries. Conflicts also affect their neighboring countries, who may struggle to cope with the consequences of massive displacement and refugee flows.

If we look at the trends today, we can see that the majority of conflicts are internal – although some involve foreign actors as well – and that many of these are caused by tension along ethnic or ideological lines. For example, in Asia subnational conflicts fought along the lines of ethnicity, religion, and geography are the most widespread and enduring form of conflict affecting the region. These occur in spite of high economic growth – for example in countries like Indonesia, Thailand, Myanmar, and the Philippines.

One of the most worrying trends in many of today's crises is the rise of violence against minorities along the lines of identity – whether religious, ethnic or based on gender. The RELIGIOUS FREEDOM IN THE WORLD REPORT 2014, which was released on 4 November 2014, states that out of 196 countries, 81 (41 percent) are designated as places where religious freedom is impaired, with 20 countries designated as "high" risk. These include: Afghanistan, Central African Republic, Egypt, Iraq, Myanmar, Nigeria, Pakistan, Saudi Arabia, Syria and Yemen.

From the Yazidi Christians in Iraq to the Kurds in Syria, to the Rohingya and Muslim minority in Myanmar, from religious violence in the Central African Republic to the persecution of Christians in North Korea, the persecution of religious minorities is on the rise in almost every continent of the globe. This includes, as we have seen with conflict, in high and middle-income countries.

We cannot assume that tolerance for diversity and the protection of religious minorities will occur automatically with rising development gains. The protection of religious minorities cannot be achieved without addressing the fundamental causes of inequality and extremism, which are always political.

Political solutions, however, are often elusive, especially in the midst of open conflict, or where politics is framed in religious and ethnic terms. In these contexts, parties to a conflict are bound by International Humanitarian Law and bear the primary responsibility for the safety and well-being of populations under their control. States also have to abide by their human rights obligations.

Guidance for Humanitarian Response

In such situations, regional and international communities have a critical role to play, not only in providing assistance to those affected by violence, but in calling for states, non-state actors, and all relevant parties to take responsibility for the well-being of all people – regardless of creed, political affiliation or gender.

As humanitarians, we need to repeat, again and again, the fundamental principles of humanitarian action:

- That aid is given regardless of the race, creed or nationality of the recipients and without adverse distinction of any kind;

- That aid priorities are calculated on the basis of need alone;

- That aid will not be used to further a particular political or religious standpoint.

Humanitarian assistance and protection must be given unconditionally. Conditionality of humanitarian assistance runs counter to all sense of humanity.

Protection activities are a key part of the humanitarian mission, and humanitarians must recognize that religious minorities are often more vulnerable or less readily supported than other groups to deprivation and physical threats, especially when they are already discriminated against prior to a disaster or conflict.

Humanitarians must make sure that they incorporate religious minorities among populations whom they consider with more attention, due to their potentially vulnerable status. As we have seen just this year, religious minorities are often specifically targeted during conflicts.

It is critical to note that these issues apply not only to conflict situations, but also to responses to natural disasters. Where there is discrimination prior to a disaster, there is a strong likelihood that state efforts to provide relief will be discriminating.

Humanitarian organizations have a duty to ensure that religious minorities are not further victimized by being ignored when it comes to receiving humanitarian protection and assistance. This is a benchmark of the quality of humanitarian action, and we need to be accountable to its delivery.

This is no easy task in situations where religion or ethnicity is so highly politicized. In such contexts, parties may be tempted to manipulate the work of humanitarian organizations for their own military or other goals. Humanitarians also risk being viewed as being biased towards one or another group. Sometimes humanitarians themselves become targets of violence.

Finally, humanitarian actors must approach conflicts with humility. We must recognize that we are not in a position to address all needs, and above all that humanitarian action will not provide an end to the conflict itself – a necessary condition to end suffering. This humility includes recognizing that humanitarian actors cannot do everything and that:

- Respect of International Humanitarian Law can only be done by the parties to a conflict;

- Solving and prevention of conflicts requires political action;

- Solving poverty is key and requires sustainable development ultimately led by the government;

- Building peace requires the expertise of the peace building community.

So, what can we do?

First and foremost, we can, and must, constantly reinforce principled humanitarian action in conflicts. We can ensure that all of our actions adhere to the four fundamental principles of humanity, neutrality, impartiality and independence. This means engaging in dialogue with all parties to a conflict, and all parties affected by a conflict, including minorities.

Second, we can strive to better understand the dynamics of conflicts, and develop context-specific strategies to negotiate access, deliver assistance and protection to the most vulnerable, and manage security risks. Humanitarians must have a good understanding of local cultures and regulations, and must be close to the people we aim to serve.

Third, we can improve our understanding of people's real needs in conflicts, as opposed to viewing needs through the predetermined lenses of our programmes. In doing this, we can improve our ability to address those specific risks to which people are confronted, and which they consider their immediate priorities. These may vary from one conflict to another, and even within the same country, from one region to another.

Fourth, to achieve the previous two points, we must actively listen. We can listen to the needs, priorities and concerns of all people affected by conflict. In any given situation women, men, adolescents, children, the elderly, the disabled, the sick and those that care for them face different risks and therefore require different forms of protection and assistance.

Often, when we listen, we realize that the things that matter most – things like security, hope, and dignity – are not the things we are providing. Pursuing these priorities may be difficult, but that this must not result in the end of our efforts to address people's gravest and most immediate needs.

Finally, then, we can be brave. It takes courage to admit our limitations as humanitarians in the face of overwhelming needs created by complex conflicts. It takes courage to adhere to our principles in the face of pressure or manipulation. It takes courage to listen to peoples' needs – including the needs of religious or ethnic minorities – and to change our approaches if we are not delivering what they truly want.

Consultations for the
2016 World Humanitarian Summit

In the lead up to the World Humanitarian Summit, we will be conducting consultations with a wide variety of stakeholders from all around the world. We will be conducting consultations in person, online, individually and in forums and gatherings like these. We need the opinions and perspectives of everyone to ensure that the next chapter of global humanitarian action meets the needs of everyone affected by conflicts and disasters – particularly minorities.

Join us. Conduct consultations and bring us the evidence that we need to ensure that the perspectives and rights of religious minorities are respected in humanitarian action. Help us reach out to your constituencies and communities to keep humanitarian action fit for the future.

We call on United Nations Alliance of Civilization to convene strategic roundtable discussions on fault line conflicts and we are here to support you with ideas and networks who are ready to partner with you.

There needs to be an Alliance for Action – leaders of different faiths who can stand up and defend the rights of religious minorities and condemn atrocities against them. We also seek top religious leaders to be with us at the Summit to reiterate our common values of humanity and common decency – no different from humanitarian principles.

We all need to reconnect through restoration of our basic spirituality and humanity.

8

THE PLIGHT OF

RELIGIOUS MINORITIES WORLDWIDE

NINA SHEA

Director, Center for Religious Freedom
Hudson Institute

Y our Excellencies, distinguished panelists and audience. I
am honored to be part of this important and timely symposium at the United Nations.

In Washington, D.C., I have advocated for international religious freedom as an American foreign policy goal for nearly
thirty years. Lately, my focus has turned to the expanding crisis
of religious cleansing, a brutal scourge threatening our world
today and one that has graver consequences for human suffering and world peace than even acts of persecution, as tragic and
unjust as they are. Religious cleansing is truly a crime against
humanity.

Crimes Against Humanity

In November 2014, President Obama visited Myanmar and addressed, among other human rights issues, the plight of the Rohingya Muslims. Though for centuries this ethno-religious minority has resided in Myanmar, a country that is majority Buddhist, their one million members are now being denied full rights of citizenship, including through the reported use of one-child policy restrictions.

Some 140,000 of them live behind barbed wire in dismal camps at levels of bare subsistence, and from there 15,000 have fled in rickety boats in the last month alone. In a report on this minority on 7 April 2014, the UN Special Rapporteur on Human Rights of Myanmar reasserted the importance of self-identification for the Rohingya Muslims, who are being forced by the state to change their official identity to Bengali. Taken together, this is a story of religious cleansing, and it is a grave affront to human rights.

Other examples of religious cleansing are occurring in a number of countries against Yizidis, Mandeans, Ahmadiys, Baha'I, Christians, and other religious minorities – as a result of extremism. This is a new, alarming trend. And it is intensifying and under-reported.

In June 2014, I had the opportunity, through a St. John's University Law School conference in Rome, to meet with Pope Francis. I raised with him the occurrence of religious cleansing of Christian minorities in several Muslim areas. The Pontiff said that today worldwide persecution against Christians rivals that of the early Church in the Roman Empire, and that there are more Christian martyrs today than then.

Religious cleansing is being waged against minority communities that have long coexisted with the majority. We are finding in certain places, the minorities are not simply discriminated against or made to conform to majority customs; they are no longer tolerated at all.

The problem lies mostly with extremist groups. These are non-state actors, although they are beginning to exercise de facto authority in certain areas. But these extreme levels of intolerance can also occur as a result of extremist influences being mainstreamed within the societies and within governments. The targeted minorities often find that their governments turn a blind eye and a deaf ear to their plight and they have little or no recourse to justice.

Beginning in 2014, Christians in Iraq and Syria have been mercilessly besieged solely for their faith by ISIS (also called ISIL and the Islamic State) with devastating results. Muslims who do not conform to ISIS' extreme interpretation of Islam are also ruthlessly targeted. But the minority communities are not tolerated whatsoever and, without tribes, militias, or powers to protect them, they have been driven from their ancient homelands.

United Nations Response

Their faith communities are experiencing a humanitarian crisis so dire that they now face an existential threat. On 12 August 2014, seven UN special rapporteurs issued an urgent release drawing world attention to the attacks against the some 200,000 members of the Yizidi community. In early August, untold thousands of them were killed, forcibly starved to death, or enslaved solely for their religion.

Less UN attention has been directed to the religious cleansing of Iraq's Christian minority, so I will now turn to them. In early 2014, Iraqi church leaders reported that between one half and two-thirds of Christians have fled Iraq over the past decade. Those estimates date before the ISIS onslaught against Mosul and the rest of Nineveh, which was Iraq's ancient Christian center, and from where, over a few weeks last summer, nearly every Christian fled – going to Iraq's Kurdish region.

With regard to Syria, Archdeacon Emmanuel Youkhana of the Assyrian Church of the East observed, "behind the daily reporting about bombs, there's an ethno-religious cleansing taking place, and soon Syria can be emptied of its Christians." In December 2013, Bishop Angaelos of the United Kingdom's Coptic Orthodox Church testified to the U.S. Congress about Egypt, stating that attacks against Copts by radical elements are not merely targeting individuals but "the Christians and minority presence in its entirety."

This means that the Christian presence in region wide is at risk, for Egypt, Iraq and Syria are three of the four largest Christian communities that remain in the Middle East today. Christians are also being driven from other places, in other regions.

Five Patterns of Religious Cleansing

Where there is religious cleansing against Christians today, five broad patterns of religious persecution are typically present.

These patterns represent practices that, while not applied systematically or in every place, are concentrated and pervasive enough to have a devastating impact on the Christian communities and they are greater than the sum of their parts. Together, used in combination with frequency, they constitute religious cleansing, which is a crime against humanity.

While from place to place, extremists are largely uncoordinated, their actions against the Christians fall into these same distinctive practices from place to place. The appearance of these practices should be recognized as red flags for religious cleansing.

These assaults, I should add, continue despite the rejection by the majority of Muslims and despite the condemnation by such prominent Muslim voices as Jordan's Prince Ghazi bin Muhammad and Iraq's Grand Ayatollah Sistani.

I will quickly go over the five points or practices, which are the hallmarks of this religious cleansing. I will give a few examples for each, although there are many more.

1. Targeted Assassination

The first is the targeted assassination of Christian leaders. These killings are almost exclusively at the hands of extremists and radicalized mobs and not by governments today.

It's important to recognize that these attacks by extremists are not occurring as a result of war itself: these Christian victims are neither combatants, nor are they hapless subjects of collateral damage. Some radical groups have openly declared their intent to eliminate all Christians.

In Somalia, for example, the vice chairman of an influential Somali religious group declared, "All Somali Christians must be killed according to Islamic law." For decades, Somalia's extremists al Shabab has killed Muslims who violate its dictates but it kills Christians, converts or not, irrespective of their individual behavior.

Again, this is a new phenomenon. One example is Italian Catholic nun Sister Leonella, who had lived 40 years in Somalia giving medical aid to the poor – Somalia's Mother Teresa. In 2006 she was shot in the back outside her Somalian hospital.

In Syria, there have been mounting numbers of targeted assassinations of clergy. An example occurred in April 2014 when assassins burst into the Homs monastery of Dutch Jesuit priest Francis Van der Lugt and shot him twice in the head. He was not caught in the crossfire of battle, but was singled out during meditation, while unarmed. He had worked for 50 years in Syria and had come to be widely beloved for his humanitarian work.

2. Forcible Conversion

The second hallmark of religious cleansing is forcible conversion. Some extremists present Christians with the ultimatum of converting to Islam or accepting second-class citizenship, that is, living under medieval dictates and sometimes paying protection money.

While Muslim governments long ago abandoned this practice, it has resurfaced in some areas where the extremists exert de-facto control. In 2006, Sunni extremists in Baghdad's Dora neighborhood issued a *fatwa* specifically giving this choice of conversion or death to the thousands of Christian residents. Dora was emptied of its Christians overnight.

One was Donny George, the former head of the Baghdad museum, who is credited with saving most of its antiquities from looting in 2003. He told me that he fled with his family after receiving a letter restating the threat and containing a bullet. He later died in exile.

This pattern was repeated this past year in Syria, as well as in Iraq. An Orthodox cleric described conversions taking place in towns taken by rebels, in the Christian valley outside Homs:

They are ruled by newly appeared Emirs, and these Christians who are not able to flee these places were obligated to pay jizya – that's the protection money – and Christian women must hide their faces like Muslim women. If they don't pay the jizya they are simply killed.

In Raqqa, in northern Syria, ISIS created a mini-state there and issued a detailed, written *dhimma* contract, which 20 Christian leaders were forced to sign. That is now posted on the Internet where you can see it along with their blurred signatures.

In this contract, these Christians agreed to abide by Caliph Umar's purported 7th century rules for "People of the Book," including all sorts of restrictions on their public practice of religion as well as certain humiliations like not praying loud enough inside their homes for Muslims outside to hear it. They also must pay a specified jizya in golden dinars. The contract stated if these rules are kept, they have the *dhimma*, protection, and won't be harmed. If they are broken, they will be considered combatants and will be "put to the sword."

In Nineveh, Christian homes were marked with the Arabic letter nun or "N" for "Nazarene," meaning Christian, and their residents were told to convert, pay a protection tax or die. Everyone who could, fled, and today over 120,000 destitute Christians are displaced in Erbil and Dohuk. They have been stripped of their homes, their possessions and their future. Meanwhile, their government failed to protect them and even now has not come to their aid. They are living in nylon tents, public schools and unfinished buildings – wholly dependent on private charity and international aid.

Forcible conversion is ruthlessly being applied in northern Nigeria by Boko Haram. I have interviewed several survivors who told me that that this extremist group will storm a Christian area and systematically go from home to home demanding every man convert to Islam on the spot. They kill those who refuse.

Habila Adamu was the sole male survivor of such an attack in 2012 in a neighbourhood in Borno state. He told me that Boko Haram extremists shot him in the head and left him for dead when he refused to denounce his Christianity. The next morning, his wife took him to the hospital where he was treated and x-rayed, which supports his story. (He showed me the x-rays).

I also interviewed Deborah Peter, a young girl from Borno, whose father and brother were shot to death in front of her in their living room. They were killed, when the extremists demanded their acceptance of Islam. Her father began chanting, "Jesus," in response.

Boko Haram has murdered many whom it perceives as resisting its strict version of *Shari'a,* including Muslims, and there has been a horrific attack on a boys' school in Yobe – killing scores of students, who were all Muslim, because they defied Boko Haram's injunction against modern education. (the name Boko Haram means "Western education is a sin.").

But Christians cannot be tolerated at all. Boko Haram's leader said on a YouTube video that

> *You Christians should know that Jesus is not the Son of God. This religion of Christianity that you're practicing is not the religion of God. It's paganism. We're trying to coerce you to embrace Islam because that is what God instructed us to do.*

This purports to be a theological justification for their actions, and it is not justified in terms of a protest against the poor delivery of government services, as some have maintained.

3. Abductions

The third practice is abductions. A high-profile case was that of the two Orthodox bishops in Syria, but many thousands of ordinary Christians in Syria and Iraq are victimized by this.

In April 2014, we saw Boko Haram abduct 276 Nigerian school girls, 85 percent of whom are said to be Christian. Boko Haram's leader announced last week that the girls are now all married to Muslim husbands, have converted to Islam, and have already memorized two chapters of the Quran.

The abduction of women and girls is becoming a common practice, not only in Nigeria but in Egypt, Pakistan, and elsewhere.

The Catholic Vicar General of the diocese in Punjab, in Pakistan, said cases like these occur daily in Punjab.

4. Attacks on Churches

A fourth practice, and this is a new phenomenon, is the targeted attack on churches. This pattern received world attention in Iraq in 2004, with the coordinated bombings of several Baghdad churches by extremists.

Between then and 9 June 2014 over 70 Iraqi churches had been destroyed by extremist groups. Some churches, like Baghdad's Chaldean Catholic church, Our Lady of Perpetual Help, that was attacked by suicide bombers in October 2010, were full of worshippers.

Since June 2014, ISIS has destroyed or converted into mosques all the churches, of all faith traditions, in Mosul, according to Chaldean Catholic Patriarch Sako.

Similar attacks occur in northern Nigeria, where, over the past several years, Boko Haram has deliberately destroyed several hundred churches, and at least four mosques. These attacks have occurred on Christmas, on Easter, on subsequent Sundays, and they have killed many people.

Egypt saw scores of its churches over a two-day period attacked in August 2013 by Muslim mobs, scapegoating Copts for the overthrow of the Muslim Brotherhood government. As my colleague Egyptian scholar Samuel Tadros has noted, it was the largest single attack on the Coptic Church in 700 years.

Pakistan saw its first attack on a church full of worshippers in September 2013; it was an Anglican church hit by an extremist group, killing 80 worshippers.

5. *Punishing Apostasy & Blasphemy*

The fifth practice is the punishing of apostasy and blasphemy. My colleague Paul Marshall and I authored a book about this phenomenon, published by Oxford University Press, entitled SILENCED: HOW APOSTASY & BLASPHEMY CODES ARE CHOKING FREEDOM WORLDWIDE. It shows how this is a practice that is actually being applied by some governments, as well as by extremist groups in the Muslim world. We were honored that Indonesia's former president, the late Abdurrahman Wahid, who led the world's largest Islamic organization, Nahdlatul Ulama, wrote the Foreword to our book.

Blasphemy bans are being applied in novel and ever-expanding ways. State laws against blasphemy empower extremists within society and they ultimately work to suppress the very voices who seek to reconcile the Muslim world with modern pluralism – like the Dean of the Islamic Affairs Department of Karachi University who was gunned down this fall.

Christians, as well as Ahmnadiya Muslims, are disproportionately prosecuted by the state and punished extra-judicially for blasphemy in Pakistan. There is a Catholic woman in Pakistan on death row for blasphemy – Asia Bibi, a mother of five. She was convicted without any evidence. Another Christian couple was thrown into a brick kiln and burned in a pogrom whipped up by allegations of blasphemy. Pakistan's blasphemy laws have become a license to kill.

Conclusion

Targeting minorities for execution, forcible conversion, abduction, destruction of their houses of worship, apostasy and blasphemy punishments – it may seem obvious that these patterns of extreme intolerance lead to religious cleansing. Yet the international community has been very slow to identify this, to distinguish these practices from their context of general conflict, terror and oppression, and to acknowledge that the combined effect is a crime against humanity.

There is a real possibility that, when political stability returns to Iraq, for example, its Yizidi and Christian communities will have been largely eradicated. This is a grave human rights violation and it is a threat to peace. As one Chaldean bishop from Iraq lamented, this means the end of an old experience of living together.

There is much that the United Nations should do to help address this emerging human rights crisis. The special rapporteurs on minorities and religious freedom should undertake more reporting on campaigns of religious cleansing against religious minorities. They must begin with a framework for understanding the unique human rights challenges – the red flags I discussed – faced by the minorities in an age of rising extremism.

All appropriate U.N. bodies should encourage host governments to provide greater protection and aid to affected minority communities. Education that furthers – and not thwarts – religious tolerance should be advanced.

9

PROTECTING RELIGIOUS MINORITIES
FROM GENOCIDE

MR. ADAMA DIENG

Special Adviser of the United Nations Secretary-General
on the Prevention of Genocide (Delivered by Simona Cruciani)

I would like to express my gratitude to the Alliance of Civilizations for organizing this very important event and to all of you who have taken the time to participate in it.

Distinguished guests, according to the first pillar of the responsibility to protect principle, States are responsible for protecting their populations from genocide, war crimes, crimes against humanity and ethnic cleansing, as well as their incitement. The word "populations" refers to all people living within a State's territory, whether citizens or not, and including national, ethnic, religious, and linguistic minorities.

This is very much in line with Article one of the DECLARATION ON THE RIGHTS OF PERSONS BELONGING TO NATIONAL OR ETHNIC, RELIGIOUS AND LINGUISTIC MINORITIES, according to which "the primary duty of States in relation to religious minorities is to protect their fundamental rights and security and ensure that State actors themselves are not contributing to the insecurity of these minorities."

Regrettably, reports from around the world reveal that religious minorities are often marginalized, stigmatized and discriminated against. As a matter of fact, religious minorities often find themselves in conditions of structural vulnerability which can lead to a vicious cycle of discrimination, hostility, insecurity and violence.

In some countries, religious minorities may be at significantly greater risk of arbitrary arrest and detention on the basis of their religion, their legitimate religious or social functions, their activities to claim their rights, or protest against unfair or discriminatory treatment. Also, persons belonging to religious minorities may be individually targeted or face insecurity during community activities.

At the level of the community, violations include forced displacement and cultural cleansing of towns, villages and other territory of religious minorities. Furthermore, in societies divided along religious lines religious minorities are particularly exposed to the risk of atrocity crimes, both in time of peace and during conflict.

We are all very familiar with the current situation in Iraq, where religious minorities, including Christians and Yazidis, but also

Shias and Sunni, are being targeted by extremist Islamist groups and subject to atrocious abuses. The case of Myanmar, where since June 2012 Buddhist mobs have carried out targeted attacks against Muslim Rohyngas in Rakhine State, is also emblematic. The situation of religious minorities also remains very precarious in many other countries, including Egypt, Iran, Pakistan, Saudi Arabia and Sri Lanka.

States can uphold the rights of religious minorities and, therefore, strengthen the national protection structure for these minorities in different ways, including by enhancing access to justice, education and the public life of religious minorities, and also by ensuring that these minorities enjoy the right to equal citizenship, legislative protection and institutional attention. States are also responsible for putting in place adequate legislation to address both acts of violence and incitement to religious and ethnic hatred, as well as to violence, and to ensure that this legislation is fully enforced, with appropriate penalties.

In countries afflicted by religious violence, States have the responsibility not only to ensure the physical protection of religious minorities, but also to monitor non-State actors that might incite religious intolerance or violence, to establish relevant oversight procedures over the security forces, and to train Government actors. In addition, in situations of conflicts involving religious minorities in which emergency laws, military courts or special security arrangements are in place, States have to take particular care to ensure that the rights of religious minorities are protected in the context of these special security measures.

I firmly believe that protecting the rights of religious minorities and establishing dedicated minority-rights mechanisms serves to promote social stability and cohesion and to build resilience to atrocity crimes. In this context, States have an obligation to prevent, investigate and punish acts of violence against members of religious minorities, regardless of the perpetrator. Failure to do so can lead to repeated and more severe violations, which can in turn culminate in atrocity crimes against specific religious minorities.

In addition, as atrocity crimes against religious minorities are often perpetrated in the context of inter-religious violence, I believe that preventing religious tensions from escalating to the point of violence is essential to protect religious minorities. In polarized societies, those who have influence over the population – including religious leaders - can fan flames of resentment or frustration to incite their followers to violence. They can also do the opposite.

We in the Office on Genocide Prevention and the Responsibility to Protect believe that it is possible to prevent the risk of atrocity crimes by preventing or curbing such incitement. For this reason, we have developed a list of policy options addressed to different stakeholders – including States, civil society, the media, and the international community – to prevent this incitement.

The policy options stem directly from the RABAT PLAN OF ACTION on the prohibition of advocacy of national, racial or religious hatred that constitutes incitement to discrimination, hostility or violence. These policy options call, in particular, for States to build resilience against incitement to violence, counter hate speech with positive messages, and encourage the use of positive and alternative speech by political, community and religious leaders.

Drawing from one of the main policy options – that religious leaders have a paramount role to play in preventing and curbing such crimes – I have decided to organize a forum with senior religious leaders from across different religions, faiths, and tendencies to explore their specific contribution to preventing atrocity crimes. The Forum aims at producing a plan of action for religious leaders to prevent and counter incitement to violence that could lead to atrocity crimes and code of conduct for religious leaders during situations at risk of mass violence.

As agreed by all heads of State and Government at the 2005 World Summit, States bear the primary responsibility to protect populations by preventing genocide, war crimes, ethnic cleansing and crimes against humanity, as well as their incitement, and the international community has a duty to assist States to fulfill this responsibility. This commitment is timely and relevant in our globalized world, where populations are constantly changing and migratory flows are contributing to making States more and more heterogeneous, including in terms of ethnic and religious representation.

By upholding minority rights and the rights of religious minorities in particular, States not only set the foundations for protection structures within their national borders, but also create the conditions for social stability and cohesion to thrive – thus building resilience to atrocity crimes. Clearly, protection is prevention.

10

PROTECTION OF RELIGIOUS LIBERTY:
INTERNATIONAL NORMS

DEAN ELIZABETH F. DEFEIS

Dean Emerita and Professor of International Law
Seton Hall School of Law

R eligious Liberty is a fundamental human right, recognized and protected in international law and commitments. Pope Francis has repeatedly stressed the importance of religious freedom. At a conference in 2014 in Rome, sponsored by St. John's University, Pope Francis stated:

Legal systems, whether state or international, are called upon to recognize, guarantee and protect religious freedom, which is an intrinsic right inherent to human nature, to the dignity of being free, and is also a sign of healthy democracy and one of the principal sources of the legitimacy of the State. [Further, he said that it is] incomprehensible and alarming that still today discrimination and restrictions of rights continue for the single fact that one belongs to publicly profess an un-

wavering faith. It is unacceptable that real persecution is actually sustained for reasons of religious affiliation! Wars as well! This distorts reason, attacks peace and humiliates human dignity.[1]

More than Fifty years ago, the Second Ecumenical Council of the Vatican addressed the status of religious liberty in a landmark document supported by Pax Romana. The DECLARATION ON RELIGIOUS FREEDOM states:

> *[T]he right to religious freedom has its foundation in the very dignity of the human person as this dignity is known through the revealed word of God and by reason itself. This right of the human person to religious freedom is to be recognized in the constitutional law whereby society is governed and thus it is to become a civil right"*[2]

Earlier this year, before a national prayer breakfast, President Obama stressed that the right to religious freedom is an essential human right that "matters to our national security."[3]

---

[1] *"Pope Francis Opens St. John's Conference on International Religious Freedom."* St. John's University Law Magazine, Fall 2014. Available at: *http://www.stjohns.edu/about/news/2014-07-25/pope-francis-opens-st-john-s-conference-international-religious-freedom.*

[2] Pope Paul VI, DECLARATION ON RELIGIOUS FREEDOM DIGNITATIS HUMANAE, *on the Right of the Person and of Communities to Social and Civil Freedom in Matters Religious Promulgated by his Holiness,* 7 December 1965. Available at: *http://www.vatican.va/archive/hist_councils/ii_vatican_council/documents/vat-ii_decl_19651207_dignitatis-humanae_en.html.*

[3] Hudson, David. "President Obama Praises Freedom of Religion at the National Prayer Breakfast." THE WHITE HOUSE. The White House, 6 February 2014. *Available at:* http://www.whitehouse.gov/blog/2014/02/06/president-obama-praises-freedom-religion-national-prayer-breakfast.

And yet, intolerance, discrimination and violence suffered by religious minorities are rampant. In a report recently issued by the Pew Forum, it is estimated that three quarters of the world's population live in countries with high government restrictions or high social hostilities involving religion. Government actions that were measured include an outright ban on some religions, preaching or conversions. Actions of private individuals or groups measured include mob violence and harassment. The report indicates that Christians are most at risk and are the subject of such intolerance in over 110 countries.[4]

Since the issuance of that report, attacks on religious minorities have escalated. This includes attacks on Christians, Muslim, Erbils and other religious groups. Indeed, as Pope Francis noted:

> *It causes me great pain to know that Christians in the world submit to the greatest amount of such discrimination. Persecution against Christians today is actually worse than in the first centuries of the Church, and there are more Christian martyrs today than 1,700 years after the edict of Constantine, which gave Christians the freedom to publicly profess their faith.*[5]

Persecution on the basis of religion violates international law and international commitments. International treaties adopted under the auspices of the United Nations and Declarations of

---

[4] Grimm, Brian. "*Rising Tide of Restrictions on Religion.*" PEW RESEARCH CENTERS RELIGION PUBLIC LIFE PROJECT RSS. 20 September 2012. Available at: *http://www.pewforum.org/2012/09/20/rising-tide-of-restrictions-on-religion-findings/*.

[5] Pope Paul VI, supra note 2.

UN bodies provide the international standards against which actions of governments and individuals should be measured.

Many legal scholars have commented that, until very recently, religious rights have, to a large extent, been neglected by the international human rights community. For example, in 1993, a World Conference on Human Rights was held in Vienna under the auspices of the United Nations. Its purpose was to review the current status of human rights worldwide. Following the Conference, a DECLARATION AND PROGRAMME OF ACTION, consisting of over one hundred paragraphs, was adopted by the General Assembly.

There were numerous paragraphs dealing for example, with rights of women, rights of the disabled and the migrant worker. These groups had been seriously neglected in the past as international human rights norms developed and therefore, the focus on these groups was very welcome. Importantly, however, there was only one rather weak paragraph in the DECLARATION that dealt with religious liberty. That paragraph simply called on states to respect their international obligations with respect to religion.[6]

Another example of that neglect is the decision of the European Court of Human Rights that upheld a Turkish law that prohibited female university medical students from wearing the hijab at the University. The students claimed that the ban violated their right to practice their religion. In a much criticized opinion,

---

[6] United Nations, General Assembly, VIENNA DECLARATION AND PROGRAMME OF ACTION (14-25 June 1993). Available at: *undocs.org A/CONF. 157/23.*

the Court held the state was justified in banning the veil in the interest in promoting secularism and equality.[7]

Religious freedom as a fundamental human right predates the system of international human rights that was developed through the United Nations system. The Treaty of Westphalia of 1648 is the foundation of the modern state-based system of international law. That Treaty provided guarantees of religious freedom to religious minorities in the member states and put an end to wars of religion—at least for that time. Of course, these peace treaties were not concluded for purely moral or humanitarian reasons. Rather, the opposing powers found that it was necessary to guarantee a minimum level of reciprocal religious tolerance in order to maintain peace.[8]

In this country "Freedom of Worship" was one of the "Four Freedoms" identified by Franklin D. Roosevelt in his famous 1941 address to Congress just prior to World War II. Roosevelt's emphasis on "Freedom of Worship" was given at a time when religious liberty was threatened by both Fascism and Communism.[9]

After the devastation and atrocities committed proceeding and during World War II, with some perpetrated in the name of religion, protection of human rights was paramount in the planning of the United Nations. One of the first actions of the U.N.

---

[7] *Leyla Sahin v. Turkey*, 44774 EUR. CT. H.R. 98, (2005).

[8] Defeis, Elizabeth. "Religious Liberty and Protections in Europe," 45, CATHOLIC LEGAL STUDIDES 73 (2006).

[9] Roosevelt, Franklin Delano, "The Four Freedoms," CONGRESSIONAL RECORD, 1941, Vol. 87, Pt. I. Available at: *http://www.digitalhistory.uh.edu/disp_textbook.cfm?smtID=3&psid=4061.*

General Assembly was the adoption of the UNIVERSAL DECLARA-
TION OF HUMAN RIGHTS. This Declaration was the first human
rights instrument that was open to all states to affirm.

Article 18 of the UNIVERSAL DECLARATION OF HUMAN RIGHTS
provides:

> *Everyone has the right to freedom of thought, conscience and*
> *religion; this right includes freedom to change his religion or*
> *belief, and freedom, either alone or in community with others*
> *and in public or private, to manifest his religion or belief in*
> *teaching, practice, worship and observance.*

The Human Rights Committee of the UN, the United Nations
body charged with monitoring the Convention has stated that
this right is far-reaching and profound; it encompasses freedom
of thought on all matters and personal conviction whether manifested individually or in community with others. The terms "religion" and "belief" are construed broadly and protect atheistic
beliefs as well as newly established or religious minorities. The
right is considered so fundamental in international law that un-
like other human rights guarantees, such as speech rights, it cannot be derogated from – even in times of public emergency.[10]

The UNIVERSAL DECLARATION OF HUMAN RIGHTS, considered the
Magna Carta of international human rights, also includes freedom to change one's religion or belief or adopt another religion.

---

[10] "Human Rights Committee, General Comment 22." Article 18 (Forty-eighth
session, 1993), U.N. Doc. CCPR/C/21/Rev.1/Add.4 (1993), reprinted in "Compi-
lation of General Comments and General Recommendations Adopted by Human Rights Treaty Bodies," U.N. Doc. HRI/GEN/1/Rev.6 at 155 (2003).

However, this DECLARATION OF HUMAN RIGHTS is a Resolution of the General Assembly and therefore, at the time that it was adopted, it was not considered binding on member states. Rather, it was viewed as a standard of achievement towards which states should aspire.

Translating this principle, that is the right to change ones religion, into a binding legal obligation on the part of member states proved difficult. There was an attempt by some states, to delete this phrase entirely. The final text of the COVENANT ON CIVIL AND POLITICAL RIGHTS that converts the guarantees of the DECLARATION into legally binding obligations is a compromise and recognizes the individual's right "to have or to adopt a religion or belief of his choice."

At least since 1993, the right to change one's religion has been recognized as a protected right under the Convention by the Human Rights Committee. More than 165 States are parties to the Convention and are bound by its provisions. However, despite this, countless persons are persecuted or even killed for converting to another religion in violation of all international agreements and commitments.

There have been efforts to draft a more specific stand-alone international convention protecting religious liberty similar to the Convention on the ELIMINATION OF ALL FORMS OF RACIAL DISCRIMINATION RACIAL CONVENTION. These have not been successful. Nevertheless, in 1981 the UN General Assembly did adopt a declaration on the subject. THE DECLARATION ON THE ELIMINATION OF ALL FORMS OF INTOLERANCE AND OF DISCRIMINATION BASED ON RELIGION OR BELIEF. The central provision of this Declaration provides:

Article 2

1. No person shall be subject to discrimination by any State, institution, group of persons, or person on grounds of religion or other beliefs.

2. For the purposes of the present Declaration, the expression "intolerance and discrimination based on religion or belief" means any distinction, exclusion, restriction or preference based on religion or belief and having as its purpose of effect nullification or impairment of the recognition, enjoyment or exercise of human rights and fundamental freedoms on an equal basis.

Although declarations are not legally binding at the time of its adoption, the DECLARATION was considered an important breakthrough. In addition to the international agreements, regional human rights instruments, such as the AFRICAN CHARTER ON HUMAN RIGHTS AND PEOPLES RIGHTS, the AMERICAN CONVENTION ON HUMAN RIGHTS, the EUROPEAN CONVENTION FOR THE PROTECTION OF HUMAN RIGHTS AND FUNDAMENTAL FREEDOMS, as well as the CHARTER OF HUMAN RIGHTS FOR THE EUROPEAN UNION, all protect religious freedom in standards that are consistent with the international standards.

Despite this DECLARATION, religious liberty continues to be a fragile right and religious intolerance increases. What can we conclude? We can deduce from these initiatives and instruments that sufficient legal instruments exist that purport to guarantee religious liberty. However, as with many of the human rights guarantees, implementation is lacking.

However, two recent developments could impact religious liberty rights; the acceptance of the norm of "Responsibility to Protect," so-called (R2P) and the development and acceptance of criminal responsibility for violating international law.

The Responsibility to Protect is not a new concept. In his address to the United Nations General Assembly in 2008, Pope Benedict XVI noted that while the "responsibility to protect has only recently been defined, it was always present implicitly at the origins of the United Nations, and is now increasingly characteristic of its activity." Further, he described the responsibility to protect in these terms:

> *Recognition of the unity of the human family, and attention to the innate dignity of every man and woman, today find renewed emphasis in the principle of responsibility to protect. Every State has the primary duty to protect its own population from grave and sustained violations of human rights as well as from the consequences of humanitarian crises. If States are unable to guarantee such protection, the international community must intervene with the juridical means provided in the United Nations Charter and in other instruments. The action of the international community and its institutions provided that it respects the principles undergirding the international order, should never be interpreted as an unwarranted imposition or a limitation on sovereignty.*[11]

---

[11] Pope Benedict XVI, Apostolic Journey to the United States of America and Visit to the United Nations Organization Headquarters, New York, 18 April 2008, Available at: *http://www.vatican.va/holy_father/benedict_xvi/speeches/2008/april/documents/hf_ben- xvi_spe_20080418_un-visit_en.html.*

However, it is only in this century that the norm of Responsibility to Protect has come to the forefront and has gained international acceptance. R2P was partly a response to the genocide and crimes against humanity, sometimes based upon religious hatred, that occurred in Rwanda and the Former Yugoslavia at the close of the last century.

In 2005, one hundred and fifty world leaders came together at the UN World Summit and recognized a responsibility to protect populations from genocide, war crimes, ethnic cleansing and crimes against humanity.

The primary responsibility rests with the individual state to protect its vulnerable population. When a State fails in its responsibility to protect its nationals from mass atrocities, other states, through the United Nations, are committed to "use appropriate diplomatic, humanitarian, and other peaceful means" to protect threatened populations. If these means fail, the Security Council may authorize collective measures to deal with the situation.

R2P involves a three-fold responsibility: (1) to prevent mass atrocities, (2) to react to them, and (3) to rebuild following such horrific events.[12] Violence directed against civilians, because of religious practices and beliefs, can rise to the level of crimes against humanity and trigger the R2P response.

---

[12] United Nations, General Assembly, 2005 WORLD SUMMIT OUTCOME, para. 139, A/60/L.1 (15 September 2005), *Available at: http://www.unis.unvienna.org/pdf/A60L.pdf.* Defeis, Elizabeth, "The Responsibility to Protect and International Justice," 10 HOSTRA JOURNAL OF INTERNATIONAL BUSINESS AND LAW 91(2011).

The Special Advisor to the Secretary-General on Prevention of Genocide and the Special Advisor on the Responsibility to Protect noted that the situation in Iraq "constitutes grave violations of human rights and international humanitarian law and may amount to war crimes and crimes against humanity" and "may also point to the risk of genocide."

The Special Advisor also urged all actors to fulfill the commitment reached by the heads of state and government at the 2005 World Summit to protect populations from genocide, war crimes, ethnic cleansing and crimes against humanity, and to cooperate in fulfilling their collective responsibility to protect.[13] One hopes and urges that this responsibility to alleviate the suffering of the religious minorities worldwide is taken seriously by the international community.

The second development that might enhance protection of religious freedom is the recognition that, under international law, individuals not only have human rights but also have responsibilities under international law, and can be held criminally liable for violating international law.

Following the Second World War and the genocide that was the Holocaust, the resolve was heard "never again." However, in our age we have witnessed genocide "again and again" – for example, in Rwanda and the former Yugoslavia in the 1990's.

---

[13] United Nations, Department of Public Information, "Statement of A. Dieng, Special Advisor on the Prevention of Genocide, and J. Welsh, Special Advisor on the Responsibility to Protect on the situation in Iraq," New York, 12 August 2014, Available at: *http://www.un.org/en/preventgenocide/adviser/pdf/2014-08-12.Statement%20of%20the%20Special%20Advisers%20on%20Iraq.pdf.*

The immediate response to the genocide was not to prevent genocide but to react, to punish-through the creation of special *ad hoc* international criminal tribunals and the creation of the Permanent International Criminal Court. This Court has jurisdiction over crimes of genocide, crimes against humanity, and war crimes and when sufficient ratifications are obtained, it will have jurisdiction over the crime of aggression.

These international criminal courts are designed to ensure that there is no impunity for most grave human rights violations such as persecutions on the basis of religion. At least since Nuremburg, it is accepted that individuals can be held criminally liable for violating international law.[14]

Persecution and violence directed against religious minorities is clearly the challenge of the human rights community today. Discrimination on the basis of religion is a violation of a fundamental human right and violates principles of equality which form the basis of the international human rights regime. The horrific attacks directed specifically against religious minorities constitute a grave crime against humanity and risks genocide.

Diplomatic and political efforts as well as legal efforts are needed to confront this issue. Since some states seem to shy away from religious liberty issues, it might be more effective and garner more support if these initiatives were characterized as human rights or minority issues rather that religious liberty issues.

---

[14] THE ROME STATUTE OF THE INTERNATIONAL CRIMINAL COURT, 1 July 2002, A/CONF. 183/9, Available at: *http://www.un.org/law/icc/index.html.*

In August 2014, Pope Francis wrote to the Secretary–General of the United Nations:

> *I place before you the tears, the suffering, and the heartfelt cries of despair of Christians and other religious minorities of the beloved land of Iraq. In renewing my urgent appeal to the international community to take action to end the humanitarian tragedy now underway, I encourage all the competent organs of the United Nations, in particular those responsible for security, peace, humanitarian law and assistance to refugees, to continue their efforts in accordance with the Preamble and relevant Articles of the United Nations Charter. The tragic experiences of the Twentieth Century, and the most basic understanding of human dignity, compels the international community, particularly through the norms and mechanisms of international law, to do all that it can to stop and to prevent further systematic violence against ethnic and religious minorities.* [15]

Let us hope that an agreed binding international legal framework can be an effective instrument to counter these new threats to peace and security.

---

[15] Pope Francis, Letter of the Holy Father to the Secretary General of the United Nations Organization Concerning the Situation in Northern Iraq, Vatican City, 9 August 2014, Available at: *http://w2.vatican.va/content/francesco/en/letters/2014/documents/papa-francesco_20140809_lettera-ban-ki-moon-iraq.html.*

APPENDIX

LETTER OF

"PAX ROMANA AT THE UNITED NATIONS"

TO POLITICAL AND LAY LEADERS WORLDWIDE

DR. JOSEF KLEE

Director, Pax Romana at the UN

August 11, 2015

Dear Sir or Madam:

PAX ROMANA AT THE UNITED NATIONS advocates for human rights and social justice at the United Nations.

We wish to express our deep concern for the plight of Christians and other victims of religious violence. The world is now witness to the violent and heartless persecution that aims to eliminate their presence in various places around the globe. We ask for your support in protecting our Christian brothers and sisters and others worldwide.

His Holiness Pope Francis has appealed for help for the Christians throughout the world "who are being persecuted, exiled, killed and decapitated for the sole reason that they are Christians." As Pope Francis has noted, more Christians have been martyred in the past two years than in all the years of the ancient Roman persecution.

We implore you not to ignore this. You enjoy a unique position to focus the world's attention on the suffering of our brothers and sisters. Examples of violence targeting Christians and others for their beliefs include:

- In Mesopotamia, the place where Christianity dates from first century AD, a population of Iraqi Christians that numbered 1.5 million a generation ago has now dwindled to less than 400,000. Ancient Christian communities in Iraq, some who still speak the Aramaic language of Jesus Christ, have been almost eliminated;

- In Kenya, scores of innocent Christians were singled out at their university and brutally murdered by militants of Shabab, for no other reason than their faith.

- In February, Egyptian Coptic Christians were beheaded in Libya by ISIS. The final words of those who were about to die at the hands of ISIS were "Jesus, help me" and the Our Father prayer;

- In 2014 in China 258 Christian churches were attacked by Chinese authorities;

- In Nigeria, Christians and others have been murdered by Boko Haram terrorists, and hundreds of churches have been deliberately burned or blown up.

This list of the suffering inflicted on Christians and others because of their faith is by no means exhaustive. Severe religious persecutions occur in Eritrea, Egypt, North Korea, Syria, Sudan, among others.

His Holiness Pope Francis recently called on the world governments to protect Christians driven from their homelands by religious persecution and violence. Following the terror against Christians in Kenya and Libya, the pope expressed fear that the international community will continue to "stand mute and inert before such unacceptable crimes," and that it will "look the other way."

Religious freedom is a fundamental right and not just an American ideal. It is a universal human right, enshrined in the UNIVERSAL DECLARATION OF HUMAN RIGHTS and the INTERNATIONAL COVENANT ON CIVIL AND POLITICAL RIGHTS. AMERICANS.

Both stand proudly in the tradition of separation between church and state, and respect for the fundamental rights of the individual.

We turn to you as a friend and supporter of these universal ideals to do what you can in your position of influence and power to speak out for those of our brothers and sisters who cannot.

The United States must take a strong stand to deliver the message to all world governments and groups that religious intolerance and persecution cannot and will not be tolerated. We must speak loudly and clearly on this matter so that the world does not mistake our silence for passive acquiescence.

We therefore urge that the following actions be taken:

- Raise religious freedom concerns directly with foreign states that persecute and repress religious believers, including religious minorities;

- Support efforts to resettle Christians and other victims of religious violence who seek to relocate safely in the West;

- Urge the international community to embrace its responsibility to protect in the face of crimes against humanity and genocide;

- Speak out and take action on behalf of those who cannot speak because of religious persecution whether they are Christians or others.

Each of us has the responsibility to counter violence in the name of religion, whether as individual citizens, religious leaders, civic and religious organizations and states.

We would be grateful to receive your response in support of our concerns and your commitment to take strong action to act on behalf of the persecuted Christians and others.

Sincerely yours,

DR. JOSEF KLEE

Director
Pax Romana at the United Nations

BIOGRAPHIES

HIS EXCELLENCY
NASSIR ABDULAZIZ AL-NASSER

High Representative
United Nations Alliance of Civilizations

H is Excellency was appointed United Nations High Representative for the Alliance of Civilizations in March 2013.

Mr. Nassir Abdulaziz Al-Nasser served as President of the Sixty-
Sixth session of the United Nations General Assembly from September 2011 to September 2012. Prior to that, Mr. Al-Nasser served
as Ambassador and Permanent Representative of Qatar to the
United Nations and represented his country on the United Nations Security Council during the two-year term of Qatar as a non-
permanent member.

During his term as Ambassador to the United Nations, Mr. Al-
Nasser also served as a Vice-President of the fifty-seventh session of the United Nations General Assembly (2002 to 2003) and
represented his country at numerous international and regional
conferences and other forums. At the same time, he served as
non-resident Ambassador to a number of countries in the Amer-
icas, including Argentina, Belize, Brazil, Canada, Colombia,
Cuba, Nicaragua, Panama, Paraguay and Uruguay.

HIS EXCELLENCY
ARCHBISHOP BERNARDITO AUZA

Papal Nuncio
Permanent Observer Mission of the Holy See
to the United Nations

A rchbishop Auza was Ordained as a priest in June 1985 and Ordained a bishop in July 2008. Archbishop Auza began his training for the priesthood at the Immaculate Heart of Mary Seminary in Tagbilaran City, in his native province of Bohol in the Philippines. Thereafter, Archbishop Auza obtained his Bachelor and Licentiate degrees in Philosophy and Theology at the University of Santo Tomas in Manila.

Archbishop Auza completed his Licentiate in Canon Law and Doctorate in Sacred Theology at the Pontifical University of St. Thomas (Angelicum) in Rome. Whereupon, after his training at the Pontificia Accademia Ecclesiastica, he proceeded to perform diplomatic service for the Holy See, including the post as Apostolic Nuncio to Haiti, during which he played a pivotal role in the international relief efforts for the victims of the earthquake in the country in 2010. In July 2014, His Holiness Pope Francis appointed Archbishop Auza as the Papal Nuncio to the United Nations.

DEAN ELIZABETH F. DEFEIS

Dean Emerita and
Professor of Constitutional and International Law
Seton Hall Law School

D ean Elizabeth F. Defeis has lectured internationally on human rights, rule of law, democracy and constitution building, electoral reform and standards for independence of the judiciary. She has lectured internationally and participated in UN fact-finding missions. She serves as an Advisor to the Permanent Observer Mission of the Holy See to the United Nations.

Dean Defeis teaches in the areas of International Law, International Human Rights, and United States Constitutional Law. She was a visiting Professor of Law at the University of Milan and held the Distinguished Chair at the University of Naples, Italy. Through Fulbright Scholarships and the Speakers Program of the US State Department, Dean Defeis has lectured at various universities around the world. She is the recipient of numerous awards including a Ford Foundation Fellowship, a Reginald Heber Smith Fellowship, and an Honorary Doctor of Law Degree from St. John's University.

Dean Defeis received her J.D. from St. John's University School of Law and her LL.M. from New York University School of Law.

MR. ADAMA DIENG

Special Adviser on the Prevention of Genocide
United Nations

A dama Dieng was appointed Special Adviser on the Prevention of Genocide in July 2012 by Secretary-General Ban Ki-moon.

Mr. Dieng has served as Registrar of the International Criminal Tribunal for Rwanda since 2001. He began his career as Registrar of the Regional and Labour Courts in Senegal, and served as Registrar of the Supreme Court of Senegal for six years. From 1982 to 2001, Mr. Dieng worked for the International Commission of Jurists. During this period he was appointed as Envoy of the United Nations Secretary General to Malawi in 1993, and as the United Nations Independent Expert for Haiti from 1995 to 2000.

A legal and human rights expert, Mr. Dieng has contributed to strengthening of the rule of law, fighting impunity and promoting capacity building of judicial and democratic institutions. He has also contributed to the establishment of several non-governmental organizations in Africa and to strengthening African institutions.

Mr. Dieng has lectured on international law and human rights at academic institutions around the world and has acted as consultant for many organizations, including the United Nations Educational, Scientific and Cultural Organization, the Office of the High Commissioner for Human Rights, the Ford Foundation, and the African Union.

MR. FRANCIS DUBOIS

**Former United Nations Deputy Coordinator to
Palestinian Territories and Head of United Nations Offices
in Algeria, Iraq, and Tunisia**

M r. Francis Dubois had a distinguished career with the United Nations. He began his career with the UN Development Programme (UNDP) in Uganda and then served at the UNDP headquarters in New York. Mr. Dubois was subsequently appointed by the Secretary General as Deputy Coordinator to the Palestinian Territories. Upon his successful completion of this assignment, Mr. Dubois was sent to Iraq where he served as Head of the UN Office with the rank of Ambassador, then to Algeria and to Tunisia in the same capacity .

Since his retirement, Mr. Dubois continues actively to advise several non-governmental organizations and serves on their boards. Presently, Mr. Dubois is President of *Le Comite La Fayette,* in New York, an organization that promotes French-American relations. Additionally, Mr. Dubois was instrumental in establishing the Pax Romana Office at the United Nations with the mission to protect religious minorities worldwide.

DR. EDWARD "JOE" HOLLAND III

Professor of Philosophy, St. Thomas University
President, Pax Romana / Cmica-usa

D r. Holland is a philosopher and Catholic theologian focusing on philosophical-scientific cosmology and social and ecological ethics for a new postmodern global ecological civilization, for the new postmodern global Catholic Church, and for the postmodern university. He holds a Ph.D. from the University of Chicago and was a Fulbright Scholar at the Universidad Cátolica in Santiago, Chile.

Professor Holland is Professor of Philosophy at St. Thomas University in Miami Gardens, Florida, as well as Adjunct Professor at the University's School of Law and School of Theology and Ministry. Additionally, Professor Holland Permanent Visiting Professor at the Universidad del Altiplano in Puno, Peru; President of Pax Romana / Catholic Movement for Intellectual and Cultural Affairs - USA; Vice-Chair of Catholic Scholars for Worker Justice; a member of the International Association for Catholic Social Thought at the University of Leuven in Belgium; and a member of the Catholic Labor Network. He also is the author of fifteen books and countless articles.

DR. JOSEF KLEE

Former United Nations Official
Director, Pax Romana at the United Nations
Adjunct Professor, St. Thomas University School of Law

D r. Josef Klee studied economics and business administration at the universities of Hamburg and Munich. He earned his Ph.D. at the University of Munich.

He started his career as a management consultant with a German trade association. In 1965, he joined an international management consulting firm in Chicago. As a principal in the German subsidiary, he consulted German and international companies in the areas of management restructuring, human resources and business logistics.

From 1976-1995, Dr. Klee served as a manager in the United Nations Secretariat in charge of various management functions in the Office of Personnel and in Management Advisory Services. Additionally, Dr. Klee was involved in the establishment of the UN Office of Internal Oversight Services.

After retiring from the United Nations in 1995, he served as an adviser to the United Nations Global Compact Office. Since 1995, he serves as an adviser and delegate of the Holy See Mission to the United Nations.

Dr. Klee's academic background includes teaching assignments at the German universities of Duesseldorf and Wuerzburg, and serving as an Adjunct Professor at the School of Diplomacy and International Relations, Seton Hall University. He has published four books and more than sixty articles on management topics.

DR. JEMILAH MAHMOOD

Director, World Humanitarian Summit
United Nations Office for
Coordination of Humanitarian Affairs

D r. Jemilah Mahmood is a Malaysian doctor and humanitarian activist and serves as Chief of the World Humanitarian Summit Secretariat – an initiative to reshape humanitarian action.

From 1999 – 2010 Dr. Mahmood was the President of the Malaysian Medical Relief Society, a medical charity that she founded in June 1999, modeled after Médecins Sans Frontières (Doctors Without Borders). In 2008, Dr. Mahmood was one of 16 members appointed by United Nations Secretary-General Ban Ki-moon to the Advisory Group of the Central Emergency Response Fund. She is also serves as a board member of DARA.

In May 2013, DARA, in recognition of her efforts in disaster prevention and relief, education, community service, environment protection, climate change, and poverty alleviation, awarded Dr. Mahmood the ISA award for her service to humanity.

PETER F. O'CONNOR

St. John's University School of Law

Peter O'Connor received his B.A. from Fordham University and has studied law at the University of Durham School of Law in the United Kingdom. Mr. O'Connor is currently in pursuit of his J.D. at St. John's University School of Law in New York.

In addition to his academic studies, Mr. O'Connor was appointed a Teaching Fellow of International Law at St. John's School of Law's Center for International and Comparative Law. Additionally, while at St. John's, Mr. O'Connor has served as President of the International Law Students Association, as well as a member of the European Affairs Committee at the New York City Bar Association.

Prior to pursuing his J.D., Mr. O'Connor gained extensive experience in the financial regulatory industry through is work with several international banks and law firms. Mr. O'Connor actively assists Pax Romana at the United Nations, and actively works with Advisors to the Permanent Mission of the Holy See to the United Nations by providing research and analysis on international law, economic policy and human rights.

RABBI ROGER ROSS

Chair of the Board & Chief Financial Officer
New Vision Interspiritual Seminary

R abbi Roger Ross received his Bachelor's Degree in Psychology and Philosophy from New York University and received his Certificate in Spiritual Counseling from The New Seminary. Rabbi Ross was the Executive Director of The New Seminary for 9 years and is now the Chairman of the Board and Chief Financial Officer of the New Vision Interspiritual Seminary, as well as the Interfaith Community International. Rabbi Ross graduated from and received *Smicha* (Rabbinical Ordination) from the Rabbinical Seminary International in 1995.

Rabbi Ross is the Executive Director of the Rabbinical Seminary International, as well as the Rabbinical Fellowship of America, International, and is a Board member of the International Federation of Rabbis.

Rabbi Ross is a member of the Executive Council of the Committee on Spirituality Values and Global Concerns at the United Nations, a member of the United Religions Initiative and the

Committee of religious Non-Government Organizations at the UN

Rabbi Ross is a Usui Reiki Master Teacher and a Karuna Reiki Master Teacher. He has a private practice in Marital Counseling as well as Spiritual Counseling for couples and singles. He performs life cycle ceremonies worldwide. He also has a private practice teaching and using Usui and Karuna Reiki.

MS. NINA SHEA

Director
Center for Religious Freedom, Hudson Institute

An international human-rights lawyer for over thirty years, Nina Shea joined Hudson Institute as a Senior Fellow in November 2006, where she directs the Center for Religious Freedom.

Ms. Shea works extensively for the advancement of individual religious freedom and other human rights in U.S. foreign policy as it confronts an ascendant Islamic extremism, as well as nationalist and remnant communist regimes. She undertakes scholarship and advocacy in defense of those persecuted for their religious beliefs and identities and on behalf of diplomatic measures to end religious repression and violence abroad, whether from state actors or extremist groups.

Ms. Shea was appointed by the US House of Representatives to serve seven terms as a Commissioner on the U.S. Commission on International Religious Freedom (June 1999 - March 2012).

During the Soviet era, Shea's first client before the United Nations was Soviet Nobel Peace Laureate Andrei Sakharov. Since then, she has been appointed as a US delegate to the United Nation's main human rights body by both Republican and Democratic administrations. She also served as a member of the Clinton administration's Advisory Committee on Religious Freedom Abroad. In 2009, she was appointed to serve as a member of the U.S. National Commission to UNESCO. Additionally, Ms. Shea played a leading role in building grassroot support for the adoption of the International Religious Freedom Act (1998).

Ms. Shea is a member of the bar of the District of Columbia and is a graduate of Smith College and American University's Washington College of Law.

DR. MARK J. WOLFF

Professor
St. Thomas University School of Law
Pax Romana NGO Representative to the United Nations

P rofessor Dr. Mark J. Wolff, KM, was a delegate to the United Nations World Conference Against Racism, Racial Discrimination, Xenophobia and related Intolerance, in Durban, South Africa.

Professor Wolff received his BA from Wadhams Hall Seminary-College, his JD *magna cum laude* from Nova Southeastern University School of Law, and his LLM. in Taxation from New York University Graduate School of Law. He was in the private practice of tax, corporate and securities law before being appointed Assistant Dean at St. Thomas University School of Law, where he now lectures on Federal Taxation, Comparative Taxation, Tax Policy, Corporations, and Jurisprudence.

Professor Wolff was formerly Vice Chair of the Board of Trustees of his Wadhams Hall Seminary College, currently serves as

Executive Director of the Miami-Dade County Educational Facilities Authority, and is a member of the Board of Directors of the Human Rights Institute at St. Thomas University. He also serves as Vice-Chairperson of Pax Romana / Cmica-usa.